THE QUEEN

Secrets & Celebrations of Her Majesty

Publisher and Creative Director: Nick Wells
Project Editor and Picture Research: Sara Robson
Art Director and Layout Design: Mike Spender
Digital Design and Production: Chris Herbert

Special thanks to: Helen Crust, Anna Groves, Amanda Leigh, Polly Prior, Digby Smith and Catherine Taylor

This edition first published 2012 by
FLAME TREE PUBLISHING
Crabtree Hall, Crabtree Lane
Fulham, London SW6 6TY
United Kingdom

www.flametreepublishing.com

12 14 16 15 13

1 3 5 7 9 10 8 6 4 2

Flame Tree is part of Flame Tree Publishing Limited

© 2012 Flame Tree Publishing Limited

A CIP record for this book is available from the British Library.

ISBN: 978-0-85775-373-1

Every effort has been made to contact copyright holders. We apologize in advance for any omissions
and would be pleased to insert the appropriate acknowledgement in subsequent editions of this publication.

Printed in China

ACKNOWLEDGEMENTS

Gordon Kerr (author) was born in Scotland and worked in bookselling and publishing for a number of years before becoming
a full-time writer. He is the author of more than 30 books including *A Short History of Europe*, *A Short History of Africa* and *Great British Losers*.
He has a wife and two children and lives in Hampshire and south-west France.

All images courtesy of **Getty Images** and the following photographers: 6, 36–37, 42, 43, 50, 67, 70, 71, 92–93, 99, 122, 128–29, 135, 136–37, 168–69, 177, 187,
189; AFP: 64, 66, 118, 120, 126, 161; Archive Photos: 143, 147; Gamma-Keystone: 19, 26–27, 32–33, 40, 87, 88, 140–41, 144, 151, 152; Gamma-Rapho: 63; Tim
Graham Photo Library: 1, 3, 5, 8, 9, 44–45, 46, 47, 48–49, 51, 52, 53, 54–55, 56, 57, 58, 59, 60, 61, 62, 65, 68–69, 98, 100–01, 104–05, 106–07, 108, 109, 110–11,
112, 113, 114–15, 116, 117, 119, 123, 124, 125, 130, 132–33, 170, 171, 172, 173, 174–75, 176, 178–79, 180, 182, 183, 184, 185; Hulton Archive: 4(l), 4(r), 7, 12,
13, 14–15, 16, 17, 18, 20, 21, 23, 24, 28–29, 31, 34, 35, 78, 80, 81, 82, 83, 90, 94, 95, 97, 103, 142, 145, 146, 148, 149, 150, 153, 155, 156, 157, 158–59, 160,
162–63, 164, 166, 167, 181, 192; Lichfield Archive: 38, 39, 89, 102, 121, 165; Picture Post: 14(l), 22, 76–77; Popperfoto: 25, 30, 74, 75, 91, 96, 154;
Premium Archive: 84; Time & Life Pictures: 79, 85, 86, 186; Universal Images Group: 41; WireImage: 127, 131, 134, 188.

THE QUEEN

Secrets & Celebrations of Her Majesty

GORDON KERR

FLAME TREE
PUBLISHING

CONTENTS

INTRODUCTION

'I DECLARE BEFORE YOU ALL THAT MY WHOLE LIFE, WHETHER IT BE LONG OR SHORT, SHALL BE DEVOTED TO YOUR SERVICE.'

On the occasion of her 21st birthday, the Queen (then Princess Elizabeth) dedicates her life to the service of the Commonwealth in a radio broadcast from South Africa.

Her Royal Highness Queen Elizabeth II has reigned for six decades, coming to the throne on 6 February 1952 on the death of her father, King George VI. She is now the constitutional monarch of 16 sovereign states – the Commonwealth realms – and the figurehead of the Commonwealth of Nations, an intergovernmental organization with 54 independent member states, the majority of which were formerly part of the British Empire.

She is also the second-longest-reigning monarch in a thousand years of British history, having in 2011 overtaken King George III, who reigned for 59 years and three months. Only the Queen's great-great-grandmother, Queen Victoria, reigned for longer, occupying the throne for 63 years and seven months. Elizabeth II will become the longest-reigning monarch in British history if she remains on the throne until 10 September 2015, by which time she will be 89 years of age.

Her long reign has been an extraordinary story – one of dedication, dignity and duty, but also one of achievement, happiness, celebration and family joy. It is a story of stirring emotional sympathy between a people and a sovereign, a relationship that has maintained the enduring traditions and age-old customs of this island nation.

But much has changed in those six decades. As Her Majesty said in a Golden Jubilee speech at the Guildhall: 'It has been a pretty remarkable 50 years by any standards. There have been ups and downs, but anyone who can remember what things were like after those six long years of war appreciates what immense changes have been achieved since then'. Attitudes to royalty have also changed immeasurably. When Princess Elizabeth was born at 17 Bruton Street, Mayfair, in London, on 21 April 1926, the attitude to the monarchy was still one of distant respect and awe. Royals were lofty beings, different to the rest of us. How things have changed. The Queen now heads a family that, because of the proliferation of the mass media, is constantly the subject – and, in some cases, the victim – of intense media scrutiny. Its divorces, affairs, births, marriages and deaths fill millions of column inches in the newspapers of the world. Events such as the marriage of Prince William and Kate Middleton in 2011 have brought instances of global joy, while others, such as the tragic death of the Princess of Wales, have created moments of deep sadness that have burned their poignant memory into the global consciousness.

Although the Queen's job is one of the most public in the world, it is difficult to say who the woman behind the pageantry and the ceremony really is, for she remains a resolutely private woman, whose role precludes her from expressing opinion or displaying too much emotion. It is these requirements, fulfilled with unfailing expertise by someone well skilled in the art of being queen, that set her apart and that give the monarchy its unique position in the affairs of our country. For she is above politics; she stands apart from the

rough and tumble of the daily soap opera of Parliament, considering only the interests of the nation and the other countries over which she reigns.

Of course, she might never have been Queen, had her uncle, King Edward VIII, not fallen in love with the American divorcée, Wallis Simpson. The crisis that followed and his subsequent abdication brought his brother Prince Albert to the throne as King George VI. His first child, the beloved 'Lilibet', therefore became heir to the throne. However, not only was she born to it, it would seem she was also made for it. Winston Churchill, for instance, described her as '…a character. She has an air of authority and reflectiveness astonishing in an infant.'

Family was important to the young princess and it has been vital to the grown-up Queen. It is a joy and a responsibility she has shared with His Royal Highness The Duke of Edinburgh, a member of the Greek Royal family who went into exile as a child and lived a fairly peripatetic existence throughout his youth. By the time the young Princess Elizabeth and he were engaged in 1947, he was a dashing lieutenant in the Royal Navy. It is a partnership and the Duke, as the Queen's consort, has unquestionably played a decisive role in maintaining the position of respect and authority held by the monarchy for the last 60 years. Not for nothing has the Duke dubbed the Royal Family 'The Firm'. It works together, solves its problems together and turns a resolute, united face when adversity shows.

In The Firm, apart from her husband, no one was more important to Her Majesty than Queen Elizabeth The Queen Mother. Perhaps the Queen's deep sense of duty was born out of the example set by her mother. The onerous responsibility of being king was thrust upon her husband by his brother's abdication and was closely followed by the Second World War, a conflict that was fought partly in the skies above London. The Queen Mother, a staunch upholder of the duty of her extraordinary family, rallied to the cause. She wholeheartedly threw herself and her family into the war effort, bolstering the morale of people whose homes had been blitzed, providing a beacon of hope and continuity and, as a result, finding a special place in the hearts of the British people. The Royal Family's refusal to remove themselves from danger, even after the chapel at Buckingham Palace had been destroyed by a German bomb, involved them in a shared national experience. It would not be forgotten.

While other members of the Royal Family have experienced their 'ups and downs', as she described them at the Guildhall in that Golden Jubilee speech, the Queen has sailed majestically on, supporting them and often lending her considerable credibility to their situations in order to help them.

This book, however, is a celebration of celebrations and ceremony, showing the Royal Family at significant moments in their lives, moments that most of us cherish as private experiences, but that they have had to share with a global audience of hundreds of millions. From the first picture in the book – a young, fresh-faced queen on her way to her first state opening of parliament – to the last – her grandson, Prince William, on the balcony of the palace sharing with the world the first moments of his marriage to the new Duchess of Cambridge – we build an idea of the lives of the Royal Family and, in particular, Her Majesty The Queen. These are lives in which weddings and funerals, some of the most intensely private and personal moments of everyone else's lives, are transformed into state occasions, rigidly defined by tradition going back many hundreds of years.

Alongside such family moments, however, are the Royal occasions, the formal events that occupy the Queen's year, such as Trooping the Colour. Since 1748, it has celebrated the Sovereign's birthday, but it is also an important military event, involving the troops of Her Majesty's Household Division. Performed like clockwork with a military precision that is the envy of the world, it is one of Her Majesty's most important duties.

Another important formal duty is the annual State Opening of Parliament that marks the commencement of each session of the Parliament of the United Kingdom. During this intensely ceremonial duty, she dons the deeply symbolic Imperial State Crown and the Parliament Robe of State, the weight of these ceremonial vestments symbolizing the great weight of tradition with which such pageantry is entwined.

These ceremonies, too, have been performed by Her Majesty across the world in distant nations that also hold her in high esteem and affection, earned by her steadfastness during countless foreign tours and the hundreds of thousands of miles

she has covered in her 60 years as Queen. At the same time, she has represented Britain, either in a hard-headed business manner, championing British goods and trade with potential customers such as the Gulf States, or by fostering good relations with traditional allies such as the United States or with nations with whom Britain has enjoyed frostier relations, such as Russia. However, the principal motivation for Her Majesty is the furthering of Britain's interests.

The Queen: Secrets & Celebrations of Her Majesty is a paean to a life that has been single-mindedly devoted to the British people; a life of sacrifice, but also a life of celebration and achievement that is unsparingly documented in these pages. It gives thanks for the commitment and dignity of an extraordinary woman held in great affection wherever she goes, the responsibility of state and tradition on her shoulders, but the love of a nation in her heart.

ROYAL OCCASIONS

The life of Her Majesty The Queen consists of numerous special occasions, when the solemn authority of her office is required to add gravity, decorum and the resonance of history to the proceedings. State Openings of Parliament, State Visits and the honouring of ancient traditions take up much of her time, an arduous responsibility that she, of course, bears with great dignity.

Her Majesty is the most travelled monarch in British history and perhaps the most travelled monarch ever. Overseas visits have, throughout her reign, been one of her most important duties, boosting Britain's image abroad and helping to create interest in British goods and technology. She and the Duke of Edinburgh are also regular visitors to the countries of the Commonwealth, attending State Openings of Parliament and performing many other official duties.

In fact, since her accession to the throne in 1952, she has made 325 overseas visits, including more than 60 State Visits at the invitation of foreign governments. She has become the first reigning monarch to visit countries such as China, Russia and Korea. She has also been host to State Visits by many heads of state from other countries, welcoming them at Buckingham Palace and entertaining them with lavish banquets at the palace or at Windsor Castle. Throughout, she remains calm and dignified, representing the nation and the traditions of her great office.

STATE OPENING OF PARLIAMENT

4 November 1952

Ten months after succeeding to the throne, the Queen travels to the Palace of Westminster to perform her first State Opening of Parliament. The State Opening is the most lavish ceremonial occasion of the monarch's year. Before assembled peers and Members of Parliament, she reads the 'Queen's Speech', traditionally written on goatskin vellum, detailing her government's agenda for the coming year. Elizabeth II has opened every parliamentary session of her reign apart from two – 1959 and 1963, when she was pregnant with Prince Andrew and Prince Edward respectively.

THE CORONATION

2 June 1953

The Coronation of Queen Elizabeth II took place at Westminster Abbey 16 months after her accession to the throne. With her Maids of Honour to her left, dignitaries to her right and the Royal Family behind her, she sits on the Chair of Estate to take the Coronation Oath, swearing to govern each of her countries according to their respective laws and customs, to mete out law and justice with mercy, to uphold Protestantism in the United Kingdom and to protect the Church of England and preserve its bishops and clergy.

THE CORONATION
Royal Procession
2 *June* 1953

A smiling Queen, wearing the Imperial State Crown made for the coronation of her father, King George VI, in 1937, and holding the 300-year-old Sovereign's Orb, leaves Westminster Abbey for Buckingham Palace in the Gold State Coach, accompanied by an escort of thousands of military personnel from around the Commonwealth. Attached to the shoulders of her dress, Her Majesty wears the Robe of State, a hand-woven, silk velvet cloak five and a half metres long, lined with Canadian ermine.

THE CORONATION
Balcony at Buckingham Palace
2 *June* 1953

Having returned in procession from Westminster Abbey, the Queen waves from the balcony of Buckingham Palace's Centre Room to the cheering crowds gathered below and along The Mall. With her are the four-year-old Prince Charles, two-year-old Princess Anne, the Duke of Edinburgh and Queen Elizabeth The Queen Mother, as well as Her Majesty's Maids of Honour. Prince Philip and the Queen Mother look skywards, perhaps to watch the spectacular flypast by 144 RAF Meteors and 24 Royal Canadian Air Force Sabres.

THE CORONATION
Coronation Ball
7 July 1953

There were a number of balls to celebrate the Coronation. The Queen is photographed here arriving at the British Commonwealth and Empire Ball held just over a month after the Coronation, on 7 July 1953 at the Hurlingham Club, the exclusive members-only sports club located in South West London. This particular evening was hosted by the Royal Empire Society, the Victoria League and the Overseas League. Possibly the most lavish of all the balls was the Savoy Coronation Ball, attended by 1,400 people, including royalty, film stars and other prominent people.

WORLD
COMMONWEALTH TOUR

November 1953 – May 1954

The Queen has visited every Commonwealth member country at least once. Her first and longest tour – covering a distance of 40,000 miles – was carried out by ocean liner between November 1953 and May 1954, and took her to Commonwealth states in the West Indies, Australasia, Asia and Africa. Here, she is seen in her Coronation gown, seated next to the Duke of Edinburgh, at the State Opening of the New Zealand Parliament at Parliament House in Wellington.

WORLD COMMONWEALTH TOUR
Opening Parliament in New South Wales
4 February 1954

The Queen arrives with the Duke of Edinburgh, dressed resplendently in a white naval uniform, to open the Parliament of New South Wales in Australia. Her Majesty is dressed in a lace gown, designed by her favourite designer, Norman Hartnell, who designed her wedding dress as well as the dress she wore for her Coronation. This was the first occasion on which the sovereign had opened a session of an Australian Parliament, a task she would perform again in February 1992.

WORLD COMMONWEALTH TOUR
Royal Visit to Ceylon
April 1954

Towards the end of the world tour, the Queen, dressed in her Coronation robes and accompanied by the Duke of Edinburgh, leaves Independence Memorial Hall in Colombo in Ceylon (now Sri Lanka), having opened the Parliament of Ceylon. During her visit to the country, the Queen caught world headlines when she and Prince Philip visited a mud hut belonging to a poor farmer in the North Central Province, who presented the royal couple with a sheaf of betel leaves in accordance with a Ceylonese tradition.

WORLD COMMONWEALTH TOUR
The Keys to Gibraltar
10 May 1954

Governor Sir Gordon MacMillan, the sovereign's representative in Gibraltar, presents Her Majesty with the traditional gift of four silver keys to the fortress of Gibraltar, which she touches in token acceptance, leaving them in his charge. This visit was made against the backdrop of a territorial dispute between Britain and Spain regarding ownership of Gibraltar, but the ecstatic welcome extended to the royal party by the Rock's 27,000 servicemen and civilians left little doubt where their loyalties lay. This remains Her Majesty's only visit to Gibraltar.

MAYOR'S RECEPTION
29 November 1956

Her Majesty and Queen Elizabeth The Queen Mother are introduced to Mrs Gerald Legge at a party hosted by the Mayor of Westminster at the Royal Academy in London's Piccadilly. Mrs Legge, the former Raine McCorquodale, the only child of novelist Barbara Cartland and Alexander McCorquodale, would become Lady Dartmouth in 1962, when her husband inherited his father's titles. The couple divorced in 1976 but Lady Dartmouth married the 8th Earl Spencer, becoming stepmother to Lady Diana Frances Spencer, who went on to marry Prince Charles in a fairytale wedding ceremony in 1981.

STATE VISIT TO FRANCE

April 1957

On her 1957 State Visit to France, the Queen was a guest of President René Coty, the second and last president of the French Fourth Republic. For the visit, Norman Hartnell designed the sumptuous ivory evening dress with lavish gold and white beadwork she is wearing as she arrives at a reception in Paris. In a warm gesture to the French nation, the design of this single-occasion gown featured French motifs, including the flowers of France and large gold bees, the emblem of Emperor Napoleon Bonaparte.

STATE VISIT TO DENMARK

May 1957

Denmark was the third European nation visited by the Queen in 1957, the others being France and Portugal. She was welcomed by King Frederick, Queen Ingrid and Princess Margrethe as well as excited crowds who thronged the streets and squares of the capital, Copenhagen, to catch a glimpse of the royal couple. During their three-day stay they visited the Royal Porcelain Factory, a nursery school and the Carlsberg breweries, where her insignia was spelled out using 5,000 bottles of beer.

TOUR OF THE UNITED STATES

October 1957

The Queen's State Visit to the United States was the fourth such visit she made that year. She is seen here with her host, United States President Dwight D. Eisenhower, at a White House State Banquet, the president wearing the British Order of Merit awarded to him after the Second World War by the Queen's father, King George VI. Eisenhower had been Supreme Commander of the Allied Forces in Europe during the Second World War.

TOUR OF THE UNITED STATES
Arrival in New York

21 October 1957

On her first visit to the United States, Her Majesty was afforded the traditional ticker-tape welcome given to visiting dignitaries, sporting heroes and celebrities by the people of New York. The massive crowds that turned out to greet her can be seen as her open-topped limousine makes its way slowly along Broadway towards City Hall. She later visited the United Nations, where she delivered a speech to the General Assembly at the conclusion of which she received a standing ovation.

COMMONWEALTH VISIT TO PAKISTAN

February 1961

In 1961 the Queen paid her first visit to the Indian sub-continent, when she spent six weeks visiting Pakistan, India and Nepal, just 14 years after the partition of India that resulted in the creation of Pakistan. At the start of her two-week stay in Pakistan, the royal car was showered with rose petals, and the biggest crowds ever seen in Karachi lined the streets to catch a glimpse of her. Lahore's most famous landmark, the Badshahi Masjid Mosque, through an arch of which she is walking, was commissioned by Mughal Emperor Aurangzeb and completed in 1673.

COMMONWEALTH VISIT TO PAKISTAN

February 1961

In 1961 the Queen paid her first visit to the Indian sub-continent, when she spent six weeks visiting Pakistan, India and Nepal, just 14 years after the partition of India that resulted in the creation of Pakistan. At the start of her two-week stay in Pakistan, the royal car was showered with rose petals, and the biggest crowds ever seen in Karachi lined the streets to catch a glimpse of her. Lahore's most famous landmark, the Badshahi Masjid Mosque, through an arch of which she is walking, was commissioned by Mughal Emperor Aurangzeb and completed in 1673.

AMERICAN STATE VISIT

June 1961

When President John F. Kennedy and his wife Jacqueline came to dine with the Queen and the Duke of Edinburgh at Buckingham Palace, there was huge media interest. The couple had more celebrity status than any other presidential pair before and since, apart from possibly the Obamas, and there was much speculation in the press as to whether Mrs Kennedy's dress by Chez Ninon had upstaged Her Majesty's Norman Hartnell creation. Following President Kennedy's assassination in 1962, the Queen was unable to attend his funeral, as she was pregnant with Prince Edward.

COMMONWEALTH VISIT TO GHANA

November 1961

Although the former British colony of Ghana – granted independence in 1957 – was now a republic, the Queen and the Duke of Edinburgh received a rapturous welcome when they arrived in the capital Accra in November 1961. In searing heat, 350,000 cheering Ghanaians lined the route from the airport as President Kwame Nkrumah accompanied them into the city. During the tour, the royal party reviewed the army of this young country, attended a surf-boat regatta and exchanged gifts with Ashanti chiefs, as shown in this picture.

COMMONWEALTH BANQUET

13 September 1962

The Queen is pictured with Commonwealth Ministers at a banquet at Buckingham Palace. From left to right the group includes: standing, Rashidi Kawawa (Tanganyika), Dr Eric Williams (Trinidad), Sir Milton Margai (Sierra Leone), Sir Abubakar Tafawa Balewa (Nigeria), Sir Alexander Bustamante (Jamaica), Sir Roy Welensky (Rhodesia), Tun Abdul Razak (Malaysia), F.D.A. Goka, Senator Fernando, President Archbishop Makarios III (Cyprus); and sitting, Sir Keith Holyoake (New Zealand), Jawaharlal Nehru (India), John Diefenbaker (Canada), Her Majesty The Queen, Sir Robert Menzies (Australia), President Muhammad Ayub Khan (Pakistan) and Harold MacMillan (Britain).

STATE VISIT
TO ETHIOPIA

February 1965

The Queen's visit to Ethiopia was the first by a British monarch. To meet her at the airport was the 'Lion of Judah', Emperor Haile Selassie, who could trace his ancestry back to the Queen of Sheba. Her Majesty was cheered by large crowds, many of whom had travelled from remote areas of the country in order to welcome the royal visitor. Seen with the Queen, overlooking the waterfalls of the Blue Nile at Gondar, the emperor spent a number of years in exile in Britain following the Italian invasion of Ethiopia in 1936.

DEDICATION OF
JFK MEMORIAL

14 May 1965

The British memorial to assassinated United States President John F. Kennedy, consisting of a garden and a Portland stone memorial tablet inscribed with a quote by the late president, was dedicated jointly by the Queen and Jacqueline Kennedy prior to a reception for the Kennedy family at Windsor Castle. The area of ground on which the memorial stands was gifted to the United States by the people of Britain. Seen shaking Her Majesty's hand is the President and Mrs Kennedy's son, the late John Fitzgerald Kennedy Jr.

STATE OPENING
OF PARLIAMENT

31 October 1967

The Queen and the Duke of Edinburgh are joined by their two older children, Prince Charles and Princess Anne, at the State Opening of Parliament. At a State Opening, the royal party arrive at the Palace of Westminster in a horse-drawn coach, entering through Sovereign's Entrance under the Victoria Tower. The Royal Standard is raised, replacing the Union Flag. In the Robing Chamber, the Queen dons the Robe of State and the Imperial State Crown, before proceeding through the Royal Gallery to the House of Lords to deliver the Queen's Speech.

INVESTITURE OF PRINCE CHARLES

1 July 1969

In a ceremony dating back to 1301, the Queen formally invests Prince Charles, as heir to the British throne, with the title of Prince of Wales at Caernarfon Castle. The coronet worn by the prince was made for the 1969 investiture. It replaced the Coronet of George, Prince of Wales, made for the future George V, which had been taken to France by Edward VIII when he went into exile in 1936 as Duke of Windsor. Prince Charles spent the 10 weeks prior to the ceremony learning about Welsh culture and language.

GHILLIES' BALL AT BALMORAL

Summer 1972

The Castle Ballroom, the largest room in Balmoral Castle, is still much used by the Royal Family. One such occasion is the Ghillies' Ball, held every year during the Queen's summer stay at the castle. By way of thanks, she invites castle staff as well as other guests to the Ghillies' Ball. The Queen and the Duke of Edinburgh, who always wears a kilt, traditionally start the evening by dancing an Eightsome Reel with six other couples.

COMMONWEALTH VISIT TO MAURITIUS

March 1972

When she acceded to the throne on the death of her father, Queen Elizabeth II inherited the position and title of Head of the Commonwealth. In that capacity, she has travelled to every country within the Commonwealth of Nations apart from two of this intergovernmental organization's most recent members, Cameroon and Rwanda. This picture, which was taken for use during her and the Duke of Edinburgh's Silver Wedding celebrations, shows Her Majesty after the State Opening of the Parliament of Mauritius in the country's capital, Port Louis.

FUNERAL OF THE DUKE OF WINDSOR

5 June 1972

The Duke of Windsor who, as Edward VIII, had abdicated the British throne in 1936, died at his home in Paris on 28 May 1972, a month before his 78th birthday. His body was returned to Britain, lying in state in St George's Chapel at Windsor Castle before being interred in the Royal Burial Ground at Frogmore. The Queen is seen leaving the funeral service at St George's Chapel with the Queen Mother, Prince Philip and the woman for whom Edward gave up his crown, the Duchess of Windsor, Wallis Warfield Simpson.

STATE VISIT TO THE UNITED STATES

July 1976

The Queen and Prince Philip made a special visit to the United States in 1976 in order to tour the country and to attend the bicentennial festivities celebrating the Declaration of Independence with the 38th President of the United States, Gerald Ford, and his wife, Betty. On board the Royal Yacht *Britannia*, they visited Philadelphia, Virginia, New York, Connecticut and Massachusetts as well as Washington, D.C. where the Queen is seen dancing with the President during a ball at the White House.

STATE VISIT TO THE UNITED STATES
Attending a State Banquet
7 July 1976

At the state banquet held during the Queen's visit to the United States to commemorate the bicentenary of the Declaration of Independence, Her Majesty wore the Grand Duchess Vladimir's tiara. Made for the aunt of the last Russian Tsar Nicholas II, this beautiful tiara was smuggled out of Russia during the Revolution by a British diplomat. In 1921 it was sold by the Grand Duchess's daughter, Princess Nicholas of Greece, to Queen Mary. It was inherited by the Queen in 1953 on Queen Mary's death.

STATE VISIT TO NEW ZEALAND

February–March 1977

The 1977 State Visit to New Zealand formed part of Her Majesty's South Pacific Jubilee Tour, commemorating 25 years on the throne. The tour took her and Prince Philip to island nations such as Fiji and Tonga, followed by longer stays in New Zealand and Australia, before finishing up in Papua New Guinea. She had been the first reigning monarch to visit New Zealand during her 1953–54 global tour and this was her fifth visit. The royal couple are seen here at the State Opening of the New Zealand Parliament in Wellington.

STATE VISIT TO GERMANY

May 1978

In 1965, at the height of the Cold War, the Queen was the first British monarch in more than half a century to visit Germany with a trip to West Berlin. On her second State Visit, a five-day stay, she indulged in frequent walkabouts that were enthusiastically received by West Germans gathered to greet her. Prince Philip told the West German Ambassador to Britain that during a walkabout he had spoken to two women who had made the dangerous journey to West Berlin from the German Democratic Republic especially for the occasion.

TOUR OF THE GULF STATES

February–March 1979

The Queen flew to the Gulf by Concorde in order to show off the latest in British technology. She spent three weeks visiting Kuwait, Bahrain, Saudi Arabia, Qatar, the United Arab Emirates and Oman, and everywhere she went she was showered with lavish gifts. This trip to a Muslim region attracted huge media attention, especially as Iran's Islamic Revolution was little more than a month old and there was concern about how a female monarch might be welcomed in this patriarchy. There was nothing to fear – the trip was an enormous success.

THE GARTER CEREMONY

16 June 1980

The Most Noble Order of the Garter, founded in 1348, is the highest order of chivalry in Britain, although membership is limited to the sovereign, the Prince of Wales and no more than 24 other members, or Companions. The bestowal of the honour is one of the Monarch's few remaining personal gestures. Every June the Garter Ceremony is held at St George's Chapel at Windsor Castle, and the Queen is seen here leaving the chapel on a windy day, smiling as she tries to hold onto her hat.

AMERICAN STATE VISIT

June 1982

When he came to Britain in 1982 in order to address the British Parliament in the Royal Gallery of the Palace of Westminster, Ronald Reagan, the 40th President of the United States, stayed at Windsor Castle with his wife, Nancy. The Queen and the former film star hit it off, as can be seen by their smiles in this picture taken during a banquet in the President's honour at Windsor Castle. They also rode together in Windsor Great Park. Princess Margaret is seated on the President's right.

ROYAL TOUR OF THE UNITED STATES

February–March 1983

Following a visit to Mexico in February 1983, Her Majesty made the third visit of her reign to the United States, touring the West Coast on the Royal Yacht *Britannia*. One notable event was a star-studded dinner in Sound Stage 9 at 20th Century Fox studios in Hollywood. Amongst the stars in attendance were Fred Astaire, Michael Caine and George Burns. She met President Reagan at Santa Barbara airport before travelling with him to his ranch. Sadly, however, rain prevented them riding together again.

D-DAY CELEBRATIONS

6 June 1984

The celebration marking the 40th anniversary of the D-Day landings brought together leaders of many of the countries that fought in that conflict. The ceremony was held on Utah Beach, one of the landing places in Normandy in France. In this photograph the Queen, standing in the centre, can be seen with (from left to right) King Baudouin of the Belgians, President Mitterand of France, the Grand Duke of Luxembourg and the United States President, Ronald Reagan.

SERVICE OF ST MICHAEL AND ST GEORGE

12 July 1984

A Royal Page holds the train of the Queen's cloak as she arrives at St Paul's Cathedral for the service of St Michael and St George. The Most Distinguished Order of Saint Michael and Saint George is a chivalric order – the sixth most senior in the British honours system – established in 1818 by George, Prince Regent, later George IV. Men and women who render extraordinary or important non-military service in a foreign country, such as ambassadors, are appointed to the Order.

STATE VISIT TO CHINA

October 1986

In Tiananmen Square, the Queen inspects a guard of honour with Chinese President Li Xiannian during her historic 1986 State Visit to China, the first by a reigning British monarch. The diplomatically critical visit came soon after negotiations to return Hong Kong to China. While she was there, Her Majesty was given privileged access to the newly excavated army of terracotta warriors. She also hosted a lunch for Deng Xiaoping, veteran leader of China's Communist Party, as well as a banquet for President Li Xiannian and his government.

STATE OPENING OF PARLIAMENT

25 June 1987

Attending the State Opening of Parliament, Her Majesty is seen processing through the Royal Gallery from the Robing Chamber to the House of Lords, the Duke of Edinburgh behind her and a peer carrying the Sword of State to her left. She wears the Imperial State Crown. Before a State Opening, the crown is transported to the Palace of Westminster, along with other crown jewels, in its own carriage. It stands 31.5 centimetres high, weighs 0.91 kilos and includes 2,868 diamonds, 273 pearls, 17 sapphires, 11 emeralds and 5 rubies.

ORDER OF THE BRITISH EMPIRE

17 May 1988

The Queen waves to waiting crowds as she arrives at St Paul's Cathedral in London for the service of the Most Excellent Order of the British Empire, held every four years. The Order was established on 4 June 1917 by King George V in an attempt to honour people who had served in non-combative roles in the First World War. It now recognizes distinguished service to the arts and sciences, public services outside the Civil Service and work with charitable and welfare organizations of all kinds. Citizens of other countries may also be recipients.

STATE VISIT TO THE UNITED STATES

May 1991

Her Majesty's 1991 State Visit to the United States was her fourth time there and the 41st President, George Bush, was the eighth president she had met. After being welcomed on the White House lawn by the President, she visited Washington, Arlington, Baltimore, Miami, Austin, San Antonio, Dallas and Houston and delivered the first-ever address to the joint Houses of Congress by a British sovereign. She and the Duke of Edinburgh are pictured with President Bush and his wife Barbara before a State Banquet at the White House.

STATE VISIT TO FRANCE

June 1992

Attending a dinner at the British Embassy in Paris during her 1992 State Visit to France, the Queen wears her favourite tiara, the one that appears on British currency: 'the Girls of Great Britain and Ireland Tiara'. It was originally given as a wedding present to the future Queen Mary in 1893 on the occasion of her marriage to the future King George V and she, in turn, gave it to her granddaughter, Queen Elizabeth II, when she married Prince Philip in 1947. The Queen is also wearing a diamond necklace given to her by King Faisal of Saudi Arabia in 1967.

STATE VISIT TO GERMANY

October 1992

Her Majesty The Queen's 1992 visit to Germany was her fifth such visit, although three of the previous visits had been when the country was divided into West and East Germany. Welcomed to the country for the second time by Richard von Weizsäcker, President of the Federal Republic of Germany, she visited the cities of Bonn, Berlin, Leipzig and Dresden. She and the Duke of Edinburgh are pictured attending a State Banquet amidst the splendor of the eighteenth-century Schloss Augustusburg near Bonn.

STATE VISIT TO RUSSIA

October 1994

Her Majesty reviews Russian troops on her arrival in Moscow for a historic State Visit. Although Edward VII had sailed into Russian waters in 1908 and had dined with Tsar Nicholas II on board his yacht, Queen Elizabeth II was the first reigning British monarch to stand on Russian soil. The Queen, accompanied by the Duke of Edinburgh, was a guest of Russian President Boris Yeltsin at the Kremlin during the hugely successful four-day visit. In St Petersburg she honoured the millions of Russian war dead and attended a service led by the Patriarch of Moscow in the magnificent St Basil's Cathedral.

BRAZILIAN STATE VISIT

December 1997

The Queen welcomes Fernando Henrique Cardoso, President of the Federative Republic of Brazil, to a State Banquet at Buckingham Palace during a one-week State Visit in 1997. Her Majesty is wearing the Brazilian parure. In celebration of her Coronation in 1953, the President and people of Brazil had presented her with the gift of a necklace and matching pendant earrings of aquamarines and diamonds. The Queen subsequently ordered the royal jeweller Garrard to complete the parure with a tiara, known as the Brazilian Aquamarine Tiara.

CHINESE STATE VISIT

October 1999

At the invitation of the Queen, Jiang Zemin, President of the People's Republic of China, and his wife, Madame Wang Yeping, undertook a State Visit to Great Britain in 1999, the presidential couple residing at Buckingham Palace during their stay. It was the first such visit to the country by a Chinese head of state. As this photograph of their carriage procession along The Mall shows, the President and his wife experienced the full panoply of a State Visit to Britain.

STATE VISIT TO ITALY

October 2000

The Queen is received at the Vatican in Rome by Roman Catholic Archbishop James Harvey, Prefect of the Papal Household. In 1980, she had been the first reigning British monarch to visit the Holy City, where she had been welcomed by Pope John Paul II. The visit had signalled a step forward in the forging of relations between the Church of England and Roman Catholics. This visit in 2000 by the Queen and the Duke of Edinburgh was organized to mark the 20-year anniversary of that historic first meeting with His Holiness.

STATE OPENING OF PARLIAMENT

6 December 2000

En route from Buckingham Palace to the Palace of Westminster, the Queen, with the Duke of Edinburgh by her side, waves to the crowd from the Irish State Coach, which is drawn by four horses and escorted by members of the Household Cavalry. Her Majesty is wearing the George IV State Diadem, which was made in 1820 for the coronation of the king for whom it is named. The diadem includes 1,333 diamonds and has 169 pearls along its base. Its design also features the floral symbols of England, Scotland and Ireland.

JORDANIAN STATE VISIT

November 2001

The Queen often uses the 55.5-metre-long St George's Hall at Windsor Castle to host State Visits and State Banquets for visiting monarchs and presidents. She is shown here making a toast to King Abdullah II of Jordan (standing next to Her Majesty) at a banquet marking his State Visit to Britain with Queen Rania. Sophie, Countess of Wessex, wife of Prince Edward, can be seen raising her glass at the top of the picture and the Duchess of Grafton, the Queen's Mistress of the Robes, is on the far left.

FUNERAL OF THE
QUEEN MOTHER

9 April 2002

The Queen follows the coffin of her mother, Her Majesty Queen Elizabeth The Queen Mother, along the aisle of Westminster Abbey. The Queen Mother had died in her sleep, aged 101, on 30 March at the Royal Lodge in Windsor Great Park. Following her death, 200,000 people passed in front of her flag-draped coffin as it lay in state in Westminster Hall. Walking behind the Queen and the Duke of Edinburgh are Princes William, Charles and Harry, Princesses Beatrice and Eugenie, the Duke of York, the Earl and Countess of Wessex, the Princess Royal and her husband, Vice-Admiral Sir Timothy Laurence.

NORWEGIAN
STATE VISIT

October 2005

His Majesty King Harald V of Norway and Her Majesty Queen Elizabeth II are cousins, the King's grandmother, Queen Maud of Norway, having been the youngest daughter of the Queen's grandfather, King Edward VII. The Norwegian King's State Visit in 2005 commemorated the centenary of Norway's independence from the Kingdom of Sweden. Seen before a State Banquet at Buckingham Palace, from left to right, are Crown Prince Haakon, Crown Princess Mette-Marit, the Duke of Edinburgh, Queen Elizabeth II, Queen Sonja, King Harald V, Camilla, Duchess of Cornwall and the Prince of Wales.

FRENCH STATE VISIT

March 2008

During his two-day State Visit to Great Britain, the President of France, Nicolas Sarkozy, is seen arriving in a carriage procession at Windsor Castle, accompanied by Her Majesty The Queen. Earlier that day, Monsieur Sarkozy had become the seventh French President to deliver a formal address to members of both Houses of Parliament. On his visit he was accompanied by his new wife, songwriter and model Carla Bruni-Sarkozy, whom he had married the previous month. Madame Bruni-Sarkozy's presence excited considerable interest in the British media.

RECEPTION FOR WORLD LEADERS

1 April 2009

The second meeting of the G-20 heads of state met at the ExCeL Exhibition Centre in London to discuss financial markets and the world economy. On 1 April, on the eve of the summit, Her Majesty hosted a reception for the leaders, during which the Queen famously delivered a light rebuke to Italian Prime Minister, Silvio Berlusconi, after he shouted too loudly in an effort to attract the attention of French President Nicolas Sarkozy. This photograph shows the Queen in a formal pose with the world leaders and delegates from international organizations.

AMERICAN STATE VISIT

May 2011

The Queen is pictured with the 44th President of the United States, Barack Obama, before a State Banquet at Buckingham Palace during his two-day State Visit to Great Britain. Other guests at the banquet included celebrities such as Tom Hanks and Helena Bonham-Carter and her film director husband, Tim Burton. During the visit, President Obama, who was accompanied by his wife Michelle, met the newly married Duke and Duchess of Cambridge, laid a wreath at the Tomb of the Unknown Warrior and delivered a speech to both Houses of Parliament.

CELEBRATIONS

Her Majesty The Queen's life is, of course, defined by her numerous state duties, but it has also included some delightful moments, particularly when the nation and its Royal Family have become united in the celebration of a marriage, an anniversary or a birthday. Best of all is when duty and celebration become one in June of every year when Her Majesty's official birthday is celebrated at the Trooping of the Colour ceremony, also known as the 'Queen's Birthday Parade'.

There have been many other great moments, including several jubilees – Silver in 1977, Golden in 2002 and her Diamond Jubilee, marking a glorious 60 years on the throne in 2012.

Royal Weddings, too, have thrilled the nation during Her Majesty's reign. The unforgettable St Paul's Cathedral marriage of the Prince of Wales and Lady Diana Spencer provided one of the abiding memories of the twentieth century. The wedding of the second in line to the throne, Prince William to Kate Middleton, seems to have occupied a similar place in the hearts of an entirely new generation.

As we enjoy the most enjoyable moments of the Queen's reign, we also celebrate the six decades during which she has occupied the throne.

ENGAGEMENT ANNOUNCEMENT

10 July 1947

A beaming Princess Elizabeth and Lieutenant Philip Mountbatten – Prince Philip of Greece and Denmark – leave Buckingham Palace after the announcement earlier that day of their engagement. The future queen had first met the prince when she was just eight years old and he was 13. They had remained in contact and in 1946 became secretly engaged when Prince Philip asked King George VI for his daughter's hand in marriage. The formal announcement of the engagement was postponed until after the princess's 21st birthday the following April.

WEDDING DAY

20 November 1947

Princess Elizabeth looks radiant at her wedding to Prince Philip. Clothing was still being rationed following the war and the princess had to purchase the material for her wedding dress using ration coupons donated by brides-to-be from across the country. Designed by Norman Hartnell, the dress was made from ivory satin embroidered with 10,000 seed pearls imported from the United States. It had a high neckline, tailored bodice and a short train. The design was kept secret and it was taken to Buckingham Palace only on the eve of the wedding.

WEDDING DAY
Royal Carriage
20 November 1947

Cheering crowds watch as, pulled by two greys, the Glass Coach passes through Parliament Square, carrying Princess Elizabeth and Prince Philip back to Buckingham Palace following their wedding at Westminster Abbey. Her Majesty's wedding ring was made from a nugget of Welsh gold that had come from the Clogau St David's mine, near Dolgellau. A global audience of 200 million listened as the BBC broadcast the wedding live. Around 10,000 congratulatory telegrams were sent, while the royal couple received more than 2,500 wedding presents from around the world.

WEDDING DAY
Balcony at Buckingham Palace
20 November 1947

The appearance of the happy couple on the balcony of Buckingham Palace is a feature of every royal wedding. Here the princess and her new husband step out onto the balcony while below thousands of people surge forwards, trying to catch a glimpse of the newlyweds. Prince Philip was born into the Greek Royal family but had adopted the surname Mountbatten from his British maternal grandparents. On his marriage, he was granted the style His Royal Highness and was given the title of Duke of Edinburgh by his father-in-law, King George VI.

WEDDING DAY
Family Portrait
20 November 1947

Princess Elizabeth and Prince Philip pose with members of the Royal Family and representatives of European nobility at Buckingham Palace after their wedding. Members of many of Europe's royal families attended the wedding, including those of Denmark, Norway, Greece, Romania, Spain, Yugoslavia, Sweden and Luxembourg. The wedding cake was nine feet high, weighed 500 pounds and featured four tiers. It had been made from ingredients received from the Australian Girl Guides and one layer was kept for Prince Charles's christening, while another was sent back to Australia as a thank you.

CHRISTENING OF PRINCE CHARLES

15 December 1948

After his christening, the proud parents Princess Elizabeth and Prince Philip are seen with Prince Charles, wrapped in the royal christening gown that had been made for Queen Victoria's children. The prince was baptized by the Archbishop of Canterbury, Dr George Fisher, in the Music Room at Buckingham Palace, and had eight godparents – King George VI, King Haakon VII of Norway, Queen Mary, Princess Margaret, Prince George of Greece, the Dowager Marchioness of Milford Haven, the Lady Brabourne and the Honourable David Bowes-Lyon.

CHRISTENING OF PRINCESS ANNE

21 October 1950

Princess Elizabeth holds her second child, Princess Anne, on the occasion of her christening, while King George VI and Princess Margaret look on. The baptism was carried out by the Archbishop of York, Cyril Garbutt, at Buckingham Palace. The princess's godparents were: the Queen, her maternal grandmother; the Hereditary Princess of Hohenlohe-Langenburg; Princess Alice of Greece and Denmark; the Earl Mountbatten of Burma; and the Honourable and Reverend Andrew Elphinstone – all relations.

TROOPING THE COLOUR

5 June 1952

Her Majesty rides a chestnut horse named Winston at the first Trooping of the Colour ceremony since she became Queen. It was actually the second occasion on which she had taken the salute, having stood in for her ailing father the previous year. She wears the uniform of the regiment being trooped – this year, the Grenadier Regiment of Foot Guards. The ceremony marks the official birthday of the sovereign, held annually on the second Saturday in June on Horse Guards Parade in London.

TROOPING THE COLOUR

13 June 1957

After the Trooping of the Colour, the Queen returns to Buckingham Palace where she watches a march-past followed by a 41-gun salute by the King's Troop in Green Park. She then leads the Royal Family onto the palace balcony to greet the crowds and to watch a fly-past by aircraft of the Royal Air Force. The Queen is pictured waving from the balcony with, from left to right, Princess Alexandra, Princess Anne, the Duchess of Gloucester, Princess Margaret, the Duke of Gloucester, Prince Philip and Prince Charles.

WEDDING OF PRINCESS MARGARET

6 *May 1960*

The Queen, the Queen Mother and Prince Charles share a carriage during the wedding of Princess Margaret to the photographer Anthony Armstrong-Jones. The ceremony at Westminster Abbey was the first royal wedding to be broadcast live on television and was watched by a global audience of 300 million. The princess's wedding dress, like her sister's, was designed by Norman Hartnell, of silk organza and described by *Vogue* as 'stunningly tailored'. The couple spent their honeymoon on a Caribbean cruise on the Royal Yacht *Britannia*.

WEDDING OF PRINCESS MARGARET
Westminster Abbey

6 *May 1960*

The Queen Mother, Prince Charles and Her Majesty The Queen are photographed at Westminster Abbey. Since 1100, when King Henry I of England was married to Matilda of Scotland, at least 16 royal weddings have taken place at Westminster Abbey, 10 of them – including Prince William's marriage to Kate Middleton in April 2011 – since 1900. The Queen was, of course, married there, as was her father George VI, when he married Lady Elizabeth Bowes-Lyon in April 1923.

WEDDING OF THE DUKE OF KENT

8 June 1961

Her Majesty attends the York Minster wedding of her cousin, Prince Edward, the Duke of Kent, to Miss Katherine Worsley, who, on her marriage, became Her Royal Highness the Duchess of Kent. This was the first royal wedding at York Minster since the 1328 wedding of King Edward III to Philippa of Hainault. Amongst those at the ceremony were the Earl and Countess Mountbatten, the Duke and Duchess of Gloucester, actor Douglas Fairbanks and playwright and actor Noel Coward, as well as numerous representatives of Europe's noble families.

TROOPING THE COLOUR

8 June 1963

Her Majesty salutes as the National Anthem is played during the Trooping of the Colour. The parade, dating back to the seventeenth century, is one of the most important ceremonies of the year, commemorating the practice of carrying, or trooping, the flags, or colours, of a battalion down the ranks so that they could be seen and recognized by soldiers in battle. From the reign of Edward VII onwards, the sovereign has taken the salute in person in the midst of great pageantry and extraordinary military precision.

TROOPING THE COLOUR

12 June 1965

Her Majesty waits on horseback for the march-past of troops at the Trooping of the Colour. The ceremony is carried out by troops of the Household Division – Foot Guards and Household Cavalry – watched by the Royal Family, invited guests and members of the public. The Queen is greeted by a salute and then inspects her troops. After the massed bands have performed a musical 'troop', the escorted regimental colour is carried down the ranks. The entire Household Division then marches past Her Majesty.

CHRISTMAS TIME AT WINDSOR CASTLE

26 December 1971

The Royal Family are celebrating Christmas at Windsor Castle. Present are: back row (left to right), the Earl of Snowdon, the Duchess of Kent with Lord Nicholas Windsor, the Duke of Kent, Prince Michael of Kent, the Duke of Edinburgh, the Prince of Wales, Prince Andrew, the Honourable Angus Ogilvy; centre row (left to right), Princess Margaret, the Queen Mother, Her Majesty The Queen, the Earl of St Andrews, Princess Anne, Marina Ogilvy, Princess Alexandra, James Ogilvy; and front row (left to right), Lady Sarah Armstrong-Jones, Viscount Linley, Prince Edward and Lady Helen Windsor.

SILVER WEDDING ANNIVERSARY

20 November 1972

Her Majesty and the Duke of Edinburgh are photographed on the occasion of their 25th wedding anniversary. The date was marked by a Service of Thanksgiving at Westminster Abbey, followed by a ceremonial drive in a Royal Landau carriage to the City of London for lunch at the Guildhall. The Royal Couple received many wonderful gifts, amongst which was a nest of silver boxes engraved with views of the royal residences that had been commissioned by the Prince of Wales from the goldsmith Gerald Benney.

SILVER WEDDING ANNIVERSARY
Round of Engagements

21 November 1972

The Queen and the Duke of Edinburgh, accompanied by Prince Charles and Princess Anne, leave Buckingham Palace for a round of engagements celebrating Her Majesty's silver wedding anniversary. The open State Postilion Landau carriage, often used for state processions for visiting heads of state, makes its way through streets lined with cheering crowds to the City of London for lunch at the Guildhall, but not before observing the tradition of touching the Lord Mayor's sword at Temple Bar in order to gain permission to enter the City.

WEDDING OF PRINCESS ANNE

14 November 1973

Princess Anne and her new husband, Captain Mark Phillips, amidst other members of the Royal Family, wave from the balcony of Buckingham Palace following their wedding at Westminster Abbey. The day had been declared a Bank Holiday and the wedding was broadcast to a worldwide audience of 500 million people. On the balcony with the happy couple are (from left to right) Lady Sarah Armstrong-Jones, Prince Charles, Her Majesty The Queen, Prince Andrew and the Duke of Edinburgh.

SILVER JUBILEE CELEBRATIONS

30 May 1977

Her Majesty smiles as she attends a gala performance of *Gloriana* at Covent Garden, arranged to celebrate her Silver Jubilee. During the summer, parties and events took place throughout Britain and the Commonwealth, re-affirming Her Majesty's abiding popularity. Beginning in Glasgow on 17 May, she undertook extensive tours of both Britain and the Commonwealth. In fact, no monarch had ever visited as much of the country as she did during six tours that covered 36 counties of the United Kingdom.

SILVER JUBILEE CELEBRATIONS
Royal Procession
7 June 1977

During her Silver Jubilee celebrations, the Queen rides with the Duke of Edinburgh in an open carriage on the way to St Paul's Cathedral, where the Royal Family were to attend a Service of Thanksgiving in the company of numerous world leaders, including US President Jimmy Carter and British Prime Minister James Callaghan. Also present were all the living former Prime Ministers – Macmillan, Douglas-Home, Wilson and Heath. After the service, the procession returned to Buckingham Palace, where tens of thousands of people greeted them.

SILVER JUBILEE
CELEBRATIONS
Walkabout in London
7 June 1977

The Queen, wearing striking sugar-pink, is seen with the Duke of Edinburgh during her Silver Jubilee walkabout in London. A huge worldwide television audience saw Her Majesty chatting with crowds, who had waited for hours to catch a glimpse of her. The Lord Mayor walked with her and noted that there were no policemen within 200 yards of the royal party. When he asked the Metropolitan Police Commissioner why this was, he was told, 'The Queen doesn't like having policemen near her when she's doing a walkabout. She thinks they get in the way!'

SILVER JUBILEE
CELEBRATIONS
Balcony at Buckingham Palace
7 June 1977

At the end of a busy series of Silver Jubilee engagements, the royal couple take to the balcony of Buckingham Palace to acknowledge the vast crowds that have gathered to celebrate her 25 years on the throne. Elsewhere in Great Britain, towns and villages were hung with bunting and countless street parties were held. In London alone, there were more than 4,000 organized parties for individual streets and neighbourhoods. Many places were named to commemorate the Jubilee, including the Fleet Line of the London Underground, which opened in 1979.

TROOPING THE COLOUR

16 June 1979

Her Majesty takes the salute at the Trooping of the Colour, riding her horse, Burmese, a gift from the Royal Canadian Mounted Police in 1969. Burmese is the horse most associated with the Queen, ridden by her at 18 consecutive Trooping the Colour ceremonies. Since their 1969 gift, the RCMP have provided Her Majesty with a further three horses, all from the same bloodline as Burmese – PSH Centenial (sic), marking the RCMP's centennial in 1973, James in 1998, marking its 125th anniversary, and George in 2009, commemorating the first gift.

QUEEN MOTHER'S 80TH BIRTHDAY

4 August 1980

Queen Elizabeth The Queen Mother celebrates her 80th birthday on the balcony of Buckingham Palace with (from left to right) Princess Margaret, Lord Linley, Her Majesty The Queen, the Duke of Edinburgh and Prince Edward. Celebratory garden parties were staged at Holyroodhouse and Buckingham Palace and a Service of Thanksgiving was held at St Paul's. In bright sunshine, the Queen Mother had driven to St Paul's through the streets of London in an open carriage with Prince Charles. Meanwhile, thousands gathered outside her home, Clarence House, to sing and cheer.

WEDDING OF PRINCE CHARLES AND DIANA

29 July 1981

Accompanied by a Sovereign's Escort of Household Cavalry, the Queen and the Duke of Edinburgh ride in an open carriage to the wedding of Prince Charles and Lady Diana Spencer at St Paul's Cathedral. The mounted officer at the far right of the picture is Lieutenant-Colonel Andrew Parker-Bowles, at the time Commanding Officer of the Household Cavalry. In 1973, Lieutenant-Colonel Parker-Bowles had married Camilla Shand, a former girlfriend of Prince Charles. The two were divorced in 1995 and in 2005 Mrs Parker-Bowles married Prince Charles, becoming the Duchess of Cornwall.

WEDDING OF PRINCE CHARLES AND DIANA
Family Portrait
29 July 1981

Family and guests pose with Charles and Diana in the Throne Room at Buckingham Palace after their wedding. Front row (from left to right): Mr Edward van Cutsem, Clementine Hambro, Catherine Cameron, Sarah-Jane Gaselee, Lord Nicholas Windsor. Second row (left to right): Princess Anne, Princess Margaret, the Queen Mother, the Queen, India Hicks, Lady Sarah Armstrong-Jones, the Frances Shand Kydd, the Earl Spencer, Lady Sarah McCorquodale, Neil McCorquodale. Third row (left to right): Captain Mark Phillips, Prince Andrew, Viscount Linley, Prince Philip, Lady Fermoy, Prince Edward, Lady Jane Fellowes, Viscount Althorp and Robert Fellowes.

WEDDING OF PRINCE CHARLES AND DIANA
Balcony at Buckingham Palace
29 July 1981

Twenty-year-old Lady Diana Spencer, pictured with her new husband, Prince Charles, Her Majesty The Queen and three bridesmaids on the balcony of Buckingham Palace, became the Princess of Wales on her marriage. The ceremony had, unusually for a royal wedding, taken place at St Paul's Cathedral and not Westminster Abbey, because it offered more seating. Described as a 'fairy-tale wedding', it was watched by a global television audience of 750 million, while it is estimated that 600,000 people lined the streets of London to catch a glimpse of the newlyweds.

TROOPING
THE COLOUR

15 June 1985

From the balcony of Buckingham Palace, Her Majesty
The Queen greets the crowds gathered below as the Royal
Family await the traditional fly-past by aircraft of the Royal
Air Force following the Trooping of the Colour ceremony
in Whitehall. Prince Charles, standing next to a laughing
Princess of Wales, is carrying in his arms 10-month-old Prince
Harry, third in line to the throne, while his other son, Prince
William, second in line, is at the front, on the Queen's left in
the centre of the picture.

QUEEN'S 60TH BIRTHDAY

21 April 1986

Her Majesty and the Duke of Edinburgh ride in the Scottish State Coach through Windsor during her 60th birthday celebrations. This carriage had been built in 1830 for Prince Adolphus, Duke of Cambridge, and had been presented as a gift to Queen Mary in 1920. Her Majesty celebrated her birthday by attending a service at St George's Chapel, Windsor, and then later, at Buckingham Palace, had been presented with thousands of daffodils by children who sang a specially composed song. In the evening, she attended a Gala Performance at the Royal Opera House.

TROOPING THE COLOUR

14 June 1986

The Queen, wearing her customary ceremonial dress, rides side-saddle on her horse Burmese as she carries out the Inspection of the Line at the Trooping of the Colour. It was the 36th and last time on which Her Majesty would ride a horse at the ceremony. Since 1987, dressed in civilian clothing, she has ridden in a phaeton carriage to carry out the inspection, taking the Royal Salute from a dais on the parade ground at which she arrives at exactly 11 o'clock.

WEDDING OF PRINCE ANDREW

23 July 1986

Her Majesty and the Duke of Edinburgh are driven in a carriage procession to the wedding of Prince Andrew and Sarah Ferguson at Westminster Abbey. Prince Andrew had known Miss Ferguson since childhood, the couple becoming re-acquainted with each other at Royal Ascot in 1985. The footmen on the back of the coach are, on the right, a Royalty Protection Squad officer and, on the left, Paul Burrell, who would later become butler to Diana, Princess of Wales and something of a media personality following her tragic death.

WEDDING OF PRINCE ANDREW
Bid Farewell

23 July 1986

The Queen places her hand affectionately on the head of four-year-old Prince William as she and other members of the Royal Family, guests and household staff wave Prince Andrew and his new bride off on their honeymoon. Her Majesty had conferred the title of Duke of York on her second oldest son 90 minutes before the ceremony that was attended by 17 members of foreign royalty, United States First Lady Nancy Reagan and British Prime Minister Margaret Thatcher. Sadly, the marriage would end in divorce in 1996.

GARDEN PARTY AT BUCKINGHAM PALACE

26 July 1989

The Queen steps out onto the lawn at the rear of Buckingham Palace to greet guests at a royal garden party. Her Majesty holds many garden parties each summer. Guests come from all walks of life, but generally hold a public position or have achieved something of national interest. They take tea and sandwiches in large marquees erected in the garden. The Queen emerges from the palace with other members of the Royal Family following the National Anthem and circulates amongst her guests.

TROOPING THE COLOUR

15 June 1991

From a balcony at Buckingham Palace, the Royal Family watches the annual fly-past that takes place after the Trooping the Colour ceremony. Gazing skywards are: (front row, from left to right) the Duke of Kent, Princess Alexandra, Princess Margaret, Queen Elizabeth The Queen Mother, Her Majesty The Queen, the Duke of Edinburgh, the Duchess of Kent, the Prince of Wales; and (back row, from left to right) the Grand Duchess of Luxembourg, Angus Ogilvy, Lord Romsey and Lady Romsey.

TROOPING
THE COLOUR

15 June 1996

Accompanied by an escort of Household Cavalry, Her Majesty leaves Buckingham Palace in the carriage procession to Horse Guards Parade in Whitehall for the Trooping the Colour ceremony. She rides in Queen Victoria's 1842 ivory-mounted phaeton drawn by two Windsor-grey horses. Trooping the Colour used to be even more spectacular than it is today. In 1920, for instance, there were ten complete guards on parade and in the past the monarchs of Europe and nobility from around the world would gather for the Imperial Birthday.

GOLDEN WEDDING ANNIVERSARY

19 November 1997

Her Majesty arrives, looking happy and relaxed, at the Royal Festival Hall at the Southbank Centre in London for a Royal Gala in celebration of her Golden Wedding Anniversary. She is wearing an embroidered gold evening dress, designed by Maureen Rose, which is complemented by contemporary diamonds. Her Majesty and the Duke of Edinburgh had earlier attended a service at Westminster Abbey and a lunch at the Guildhall. The best present, however, was news that restoration of fire-damaged Windsor Castle had been completed that day.

TROOPING THE COLOUR

12 June 1999

Following the last Trooping of the Colour ceremony of the twentieth century, Sophie Rhys-Jones (far left) joins Her Majesty The Queen on the balcony of Buckingham Palace. It was just seven days before her marriage to the Queen's youngest child, Prince Edward, who is standing on his fiancée's left. Also acknowledging the crowds are Princess Anne and her second husband, Commodore Timothy Laurence. He had married the princess in 1992 after her divorce from her first husband, Mark Phillips.

WEDDING OF PRINCE EDWARD

19 June 1999

Her Majesty looks on as Prince Edward and his bride, Sophie Rhys-Jones, leave St George's Chapel in Windsor following their wedding. The prince had met Miss Rhys-Jones at a tennis event in 1993 and their engagement had been announced on 6 January 1999. The couple insisted on their wedding not being turned into a state occasion and guests were requested to wear formal evening gowns instead of court dress. Hats were not to be worn, although the Queen Mother ignored this request, as she was never seen without one.

WEDDING OF PRINCE EDWARD
Steps of St George's Chapel

19 June 1999

Guests stand on the steps of St George's Chapel waving goodbye to Prince Edward and his new wife following their wedding. It was announced before the wedding that the Queen had conferred on him and his bride the titles of Earl and Countess of Wessex. This represented a break with tradition, as the son of the sovereign is customarily made a duke and Edward was the first since George I not to be so titled. It was also announced, however, that he will assume the title of Duke of Edinburgh after the deaths of both his parents.

QUEEN MOTHER'S 100TH BIRTHDAY

4 August 2000

On the occasion of her 100th birthday, Her Majesty Queen Elizabeth The Queen Mother affectionately acknowledges the thousands of well-wishers in The Mall below from the balcony of Buckingham Palace. On the balcony with Her Majesty are (from left to right) the Princess Royal, Peter Phillips, Princess Eugenie, Princess Beatrice, Prince Andrew, Princess Margaret, the Queen Mother, the Earl of Wessex, Her Majesty The Queen, the Duke of Edinburgh, the Countess of Wessex, Prince William, Prince Charles, Prince Harry and the Duchess of Kent.

GOLDEN JUBILEE CELEBRATIONS

26 November 2001

Her Majesty is pictured with the Duke of Edinburgh in one of a series of photographs taken to commemorate her upcoming Golden Jubilee. Despite the deaths of Princess Margaret and the Queen Mother in February and March 2002 respectively, Her Majesty was determined to commemorate her 50 years as a sovereign and to thank her people for their loyalty. In Britain, the Golden Jubilee Weekend took place between 1 and 4 June 2002, with numerous events taking place, including concerts in the gardens of Buckingham Palace and the lighting of a chain of beacons around the world.

GOLDEN JUBILEE CELEBRATIONS
Royal Procession
4 June 2002

The Queen travels in the Gold State Coach to St Paul's where a Service of Thanksgiving is being held to mark her Golden Jubilee. Built in 1762, the Gold Coach has been used at the coronation of every British monarch since George IV. Its great weight and size make it extremely difficult to manoeuvre and it is therefore used only on grand state occasions. The coach features panels painted by Italian painter Giovanni Cipriani and gilded sculptures.

GOLDEN JUBILEE CELEBRATIONS
Service of Thanksgiving
4 June 2002

At the Service of Thanksgiving for Her Majesty's Golden Jubilee, the Royal Family is pictured processing down the aisle of St Paul's Cathedral. The Queen and the Duke of Edinburgh lead the procession, followed by the Prince of Wales, Prince William and Prince Harry, Princess Beatrice, the Duke of York and Princess Eugenie, the Earl and Countess of Wessex, the Princess Royal and her husband, Rear-Admiral Timothy Laurence, Princess Anne's children, Peter and Zara Phillips, and, at the back, Viscount and Viscountess Linley.

GOLDEN JUBILEE CELEBRATIONS
Leaving St Paul's Cathedral
4 June 2002

Her Majesty and the Duke of Edinburgh leave St Paul's at the end of the Service of Thanksgiving for her Golden Jubilee. On the right of the Duke is the Lord Mayor of London, Sir Michael Oliver, and behind the royal couple are Prince William and Prince Harry. Amongst the many events being held in the United Kingdom to celebrate the Jubilee was a dinner hosted by Prime Minister Tony Blair at 10 Downing Street, attended by all the Prime Ministers of her reign still living.

GOLDEN JUBILEE CELEBRATIONS
The Sovereigns of Europe
17 June 2002

In the Crimson Drawing Room at Windsor Castle Her Majesty poses with the reigning sovereigns of Europe for a unique photograph to mark her Golden Jubilee. Front row, left to right: Queen Margrethe II of Denmark, Queen Elizabeth II and Queen Beatrix of the Netherlands. Behind, left to right: Albert II, King of the Belgians, King Juan Carlos I of Spain, King Harald V of Norway, King Carl XVI Gustaf of Sweden and Henri, Grand Duke of Luxembourg.

GOLDEN JUBILEE CELEBRATIONS
Celebrations in Canada
10 October 2002

Over 12 months, the royal couple journeyed more than 40,000 miles, touring the Caribbean, Australia, New Zealand and the United Kingdom to mark her Golden Jubilee. The year ended in Canada, where Her Majesty is pictured waving to the crowd following a gala concert featuring Canadian stars in Toronto. She and the Duke spent 12 days in Canada, touring extensively. Celebratory events also took place outside the Commonwealth countries. In New York, for example, the Empire State Building was illuminated in purple and gold.

WEDDING OF PRINCE CHARLES AND CAMILLA

9 April 2005

The Prince of Wales and his new wife, Camilla Parker-Bowles, are seen with Her Majesty The Queen attending the service of prayer and dedication that followed their civil wedding ceremony at Windsor Guildhall. The couple's witnesses were Prince William of Wales and the bride's son, Tom Parker-Bowles, and, in keeping with royal wedding tradition, the couple's wedding rings were crafted from 22 carat Welsh gold from the Clogau St David's mine. Although entitled to be known as Princess of Wales, Camilla chose to be styled Duchess of Cornwall.

TROOPING
THE COLOUR

11 June 2005

With Admiralty Arch in the background, the royal procession, including Her Majesty and the Duke of Edinburgh, returns along The Mall to Buckingham Palace following the Trooping of the Colour Ceremony, graced, for the first time, by the presence of Camilla, Duchess of Cornwall, recently married to the Prince of Wales. The musicians pictured in the foreground are just some of the 400 on duty at the parade. They consist of the Massed Bands of the Household Cavalry, together with a Corps of Drums and, sometimes, pipers.

NATIONAL COMMEMORATION DAY

10 July 2005

The Queen and the Duke of Edinburgh wave as they travel through London in an open car during National Commemoration Day, marking the 60th anniversary of the end of the Second World War. The royal couple began the day with a service of remembrance at Westminster Abbey, alongside a congregation of veterans and with the address given by the Archbishop of Canterbury, Rowan Williams. A luncheon for veterans was then held in the gardens of Buckingham Palace in the presence of Her Majesty, followed by parades, fly-pasts and a two-minute silence.

QUEEN'S 80TH BIRTHDAY

21 April 2006

With the Prince of Wales, his wife, Camilla, Duchess of Cornwall and Prince William, Her Majesty watches a display of fireworks at Kew Palace in London after a dinner in celebration of her 80th birthday. Earlier, there had been a 21-gun salute in Windsor Great Park and Her Majesty had met thousands of well-wishers during an informal walkabout in Windsor. In the evening, Prince Charles had broadcast a birthday tribute to his mother. Buckingham Palace announced that the Queen had received 20,000 birthday cards and 17,000 congratulatory emails.

DIAMOND WEDDING ANNIVERSARY

18 November 2007

Her Majesty and the Duke of Edinburgh are joined at Clarence House by their immediate family – the Prince of Wales, the Princess Royal, the Duke of York and the Earl of Wessex – on the occasion of a dinner, hosted by Prince Charles and the Duchess of Cornwall, to celebrate the forthcoming Diamond Wedding Anniversary of the Queen and the Duke. Events held to mark the low-key anniversary included a Service of Celebration at Westminster Abbey, followed by the unveiling of a new Jubilee Walkway panoramic panel in Parliament Square.

PRINCE CHARLES'S 60TH BIRTHDAY

14 November 2008

Her Majesty The Queen arrives with the Prince of Wales at a private reception and concert she is hosting at Buckingham Palace to celebrate her son's 60th birthday. She is followed by the Duke of Edinburgh, Camilla, Duchess of Cornwall, Prince William and Prince Harry. A televised comedy gala, 'We Are Most Amused', was also staged in aid of The Prince's Trust and attended by Prince Charles and his wife. It starred, amongst others, John Cleese, Robin Williams, Stephen Fry and Rowan Atkinson.

WEDDING OF PRINCE WILLIAM

29 April 2011

A carriage containing the Queen and Prince Philip leads the carriage procession to Buckingham Palace following the wedding of Prince William of Wales and Kate Middleton. The wedding was one of the most anticipated royal occasions of recent years, with thousands of people descending on the capital from all over Britain as well as from around the world. A public holiday was announced and around 5,000 street parties were held in celebration across Britain. A million people lined the route between Westminster Abbey and Buckingham Palace to cheer the happy couple.

Balcony at Buckingham Palace

29 April 2011

Newly titled the Duke and Duchess of Cambridge, Prince William and his wife greet the huge crowd below from the balcony of Buckingham Palace. With them are two of the Duchess's bridesmaids, her page boys, Her Majesty The Queen, the Duke of Edinburgh, the Duchess's sister, Pippa Middleton, Prince Harry and the Duchess's brother, James Middleton. The wedding was attended by 1,900 guests, including royalty and heads of state from around the world, as well as icons of fashion, film, music and sport, such as Joss Stone, Sir Elton John and David Beckham.

CONNECTIONS

Since Her Majesty The Queen took the throne 60 years ago, the world has changed a great deal and so too has our attitude to the monarchy. The Royal Family has responded to these changes, making itself much more accessible and approachable. One manifestation of this is the 'royal walkabout', a phenomenon that developed in the 1970s. It is now an exciting feature of every royal visit, Her Majesty and the Duke of Edinburgh happily breaking off from their duties to chat informally to members of the crowds.

Much of Her Majesty's life is, of course, taken up with meeting people – government officials or prominent citizens of the town or country she is visiting or stars of stage or screen. At the end of a film, opera or variety show she has attended, she is introduced to long lines of people, and at film premières and Command Performances over the decades since she became Queen, she has been introduced to many of the great stars of the day.

All of these meetings, both formal and informal, serve to connect the monarchy to the nations over which she rules, providing an invaluable link between the Queen and her subjects.

BANQUET AT
THE GUILDHALL

23 March 1950

Wearing an ermine cloak over a green satin dress, crossed with the blue ribbon of the Garter, Princess Elizabeth greets the Leader of the Opposition at one of the most glittering occasions since the Second World War – a banquet at the war-battered Guildhall to express thanks to the Commonwealth and the United States for the £800 million of food parcels sent to Britain during and since the war. Guests included Princess Margaret, the Prime Minister, Clement Atlee, the Archbishop of Canterbury, the Duchess of Kent, foreign ambassadors, Commonwealth High Commissioners and many other dignitaries.

THE LADY WITH A LAMP PREMIÈRE

7 June 1951

Princess Elizabeth was received by the Earl and Countess Mountbatten at the première of *The Lady With a Lamp*, a film depicting the life of the celebrated nurse Florence Nightingale and her work with British soldiers during the Crimean War. Proceeds from the film were being donated to the Royal College of Nursing Educational Fund. Because of this, the princess elected to attend the première although her father, King George VI, was desperately ill. She is seen beside the Countess Mountbatten, receiving a bouquet of flowers from University College Hospital nurse Jean Carie.

BECAUSE YOU'RE MINE PREMIÈRE

27 October 1952

Alexander Hall's musical comedy *Because You're Mine*, starring the popular American tenor, Mario Lanza, was chosen for the inaugural Royal Command Film Performance of the Queen's reign. The Command Performance can be traced back to the reign of Elizabeth I, and the first film performance was held in 1896 before the future King Edward VII and Princess Alexandra. Her Majesty is seen shaking hands with Kirk Douglas, while fellow American film star Douglas Fairbanks Jr and British actress Anne Crawford look on.

ROYAL GALA PERFORMANCE

8 June 1953

Just six days after her Coronation at Westminster Abbey, Her Majesty attends a Gala Performance at the Royal Opera House of Benjamin Britten's three-act opera, *Gloriana*, which had been specially composed for the Coronation. The opera depicts the relationship between Queen Elizabeth I and the Earl of Essex, presenting Elizabeth as a sympathetic but flawed character, motivated by vanity and desire. It may have been because of this depiction that Her Majesty was reported to have been disappointed by the opera and it was not one of the composer's greatest critical successes.

ROYAL FILM PERFORMANCE

27 October 1953

Wearing a beautiful dress of lavender organza, Her Majesty turns to the Duke of Edinburgh in the royal box at the Odeon Cinema in London's Leicester Square, where she is attending that year's Royal Film Performance – the Walt Disney film *Rob Roy, the Highland Rogue*, starring Richard Todd, Glynis Johns and James Robertson Justice. As ever, the event was a star-studded affair, attendees including Jack Hawkins, Gary Cooper, Alec Guinness and Kay Kendall, with proceeds being donated to the Cinematographic Trade Benevolent Fund.

ROYAL FILM PERFORMANCE

16 November 1954

A veritable galaxy of stars turned out to be presented to the Queen at the 1954 Royal Film Performance, including Hollywood luminaries Jane Russell and Shelley Winters, as well as much-loved home-grown stars such as Jean Simmons, Anna Neagle and Michael Redgrave. The featured film for 1954 was *Beau Brummell*, a historical romp starring Elizabeth Taylor, Stewart Granger and Peter Ustinov as the Prince of Wales. Her Majesty, wearing a dress of white tulle, is seen arriving for the performance at the Empire Cinema, Leicester Square in London with Princess Margaret.

ROYAL VARIETY PERFORMANCE

13 April 1955

The first Royal Variety Performance took place in 1912 before King George V and Queen Mary and starred such names as Fanny Fields, Harry Lauder and Little Tich. Eighty-three such shows have followed, featuring the biggest names in show business, from Bob Hope to The Beatles. Unusually, in 1955 there were two Royal Variety Performances, the first of which was staged outside the capital for the first time, in Blackpool. Her Majesty and the Duke of Edinburgh are seen meeting American singing star Eddie Fisher and looking on is the impresario Jack Hylton.

ROYAL FILM PERFORMANCE

31 October 1955

The Odeon in Leicester Square was once again the venue for the Royal Film Performance of 1955, showing the film *To Catch a Thief* to Her Majesty who, with the Duke of Edinburgh at her side, arrived at the cinema looking regal in tiara and glittering necklace. The film, starring Cary Grant and Grace Kelly, was directed by the great English film director Alfred Hitchcock, who attended the performance. Amongst those also in attendance were the Queen's dress designer, Norman Hartnell, English socialite Lady Docker and film stars Richard Attenborough, Ava Gardner, Kenneth More and Janet Scott.

ROYAL VARIETY PERFORMANCE

7 November 1955

The Queen meets the Russian dancer Sergei Svetkov of the Moscow State Folk Dance Company and Hsu Chu Hua, leader of the Chinese Classical Theatre Company, behind the scenes following the second Royal Variety Performance of the year, staged at London's Victoria Palace in aid of the Entertainment Artistes' Benevolent Fund. Amongst the host of stars performing were comedians Tommy Trinder, the Crazy Gang, Benny Hill and Jimmy Edwards, and singers Ruby Murray, Lena Horne and Johnny Ray.

ROYAL FILM PERFORMANCE

29 October 1956

At the reception for the 1956 Royal Film Performance, the war film *The Battle of the River Plate*, at the Empire Cinema, Leicester Square, Her Majesty shakes hands with glamorous film siren Marilyn Monroe, in England to make *The Prince and the Showgirl*, in which she famously co-starred with Laurence Olivier. Standing on Miss Monroe's right is Hollywood actor Victor Mature. Also attending were Anita Ekberg and husband Anthony Steel, Joan Crawford, Norman Wisdom, Sylvia Syms and a 22-year-old rising French starlet, Brigitte Bardot.

ROYAL ASCOT

June 1957

Dating back to 1711, when it was founded by Queen Anne, Royal Ascot is one of Europe's most famous race meetings and one of the most anticipated events on the British social calendar. Every year, the Queen, whose passion for horseracing is well documented, and various members of the Royal Family, arrive at Ascot racecourse in horse-drawn carriages, where they take part in a procession past the cheering crowds. The Queen is seen here, seated next to the Duke of Edinburgh, waving to the crowds as her carriage passes the grandstands.

GREETING CROWDS IN KATHMANDU

February 1961

King Mahendra of Nepal rides in an open landau with Her Majesty in Kathmandu during her 1961 State Visit to Nepal, while the Duke of Edinburgh shares the carriage following with Mahendra's wife, Queen Ratna. Meanwhile, the Nepalese crowds lining the streets of the capital welcome the British royal couple by throwing vermilion and saffron as the carriages pass them, and choruses of Nepalis sing and dance. During this first visit by a British monarch to the tiny Himalayan state, the Queen and Prince Philip met Gurkha troops and rode elephants during a tiger-hunt.

WELCOME IN SIERRA LEONE

November 1961

The Queen receives a bouquet from a small girl during her visit on the Royal Yacht *Britannia* to the newly independent West African state of Sierra Leone, where she is known as 'Mrs Queen'. At the Bo Durbar, a festival held in Bo, the country's second-largest town, she delighted her Sierra Leone subjects by wearing a tiara while reviewing a spectacular parade of 41 of the nation's chiefdoms, the chiefs being carried past her in hammocks. She also visited diamond mines and attended a State Banquet hosted by the newly independent nation's first Prime Minister, Sir Milton Margai.

ROYAL VARIETY PERFORMANCE

29 April 1962

The Queen arrives at the London Palladium, venue for more shows of this type than any other theatre, for the Royal Variety Performance, starring Cliff Richard and the Shadows, Australian singer Frank Ifield and Scottish singer and comedian Andy Stewart. Comedians Dickie Henderson, Sophie Tucker, Mike and Bernie Winters and Bob Hope also appeared. The Royal Variety Performance was first broadcast on television in 1960 and was shown alternately on BBC and ITV.

FOUNDER'S DAY PARADE

29 May 1962

Her Majesty talks to Chelsea Pensioners at the Royal Hospital's Founder's Day Parade in London. The hospital was founded by King Charles II in 1681 to provide care for old and injured soldiers. Its Founder's Day Parade is held as close as possible to 29 May, Charles's birthday, when the hospital's inhabitants – Chelsea Pensioners – are reviewed by a member of the Royal Family, on this occasion the Queen. Participants and spectators wear sprigs of oak leaves in memory of the Royal Oak in which Charles hid after the Battle of Worcester.

ROYAL COMMAND PERFORMANCE

8 July 1964

Her Majesty meets members of the cast of Gilbert and Sullivan's Savoy Opera, *The Yeomen of the Guard*, staged as a Royal Command Performance. This comic opera was, of course, a particularly appropriate selection to be performed for the Queen, given that it is set in the Tower of London. As its title suggests, it concerns the 'Yeomen Warders of Her Majesty's Royal Palace and Fortress, the Tower of London', the officers affectionately known as 'Beefeaters'. The performer on the extreme left of the picture is dressed in the uniform of a Beefeater.

GREETING CROWDS IN THE SUDAN

February 1965

Cheering Sudanese line the streets to watch the Queen and Dr El Tigani El-Mahi of the Sudanese Presidential Council drive through the Sudanese capital Khartoum in an open car during a Royal Visit by Her Majesty and the Duke of Edinburgh. They were treated to the spectacle of a camel race, traditional music and dancing and a visit to the site of the construction of the Roseires Dam, a massive irrigation project on the Blue Nile that was completed the year after the Royal Visit.

BORN FREE PREMIÈRE

15 March 1966

The Queen shakes the hand of British actress Julie Christie before the Royal Film Performance of *Born Free* at the Odeon Cinema, Leicester Square in London as the American actor Warren Beatty, to the left of Ms Christie, looks on. Further along the line, next to the tall figure of Christopher Lee, can be seen the American actress Raquel Welch. The hugely popular film starred husband and wife actors, Bill Travers and Virginia McKenna, playing George and Joy Adamson, a real-life couple who raised an orphaned lion cub named Elsa.

YOU ONLY LIVE TWICE PREMIÈRE

13 June 1967

Sean Connery, tanned and with a moustache, looks on as Her Majesty shakes hands with his then wife, the Australian actress Diane Cilento, at the Royal Film Première of the James Bond film *You Only Live Twice*. This world première, at the Odeon Cinema, Leicester Square, was the first time that the Queen had attended the première of a Bond film but it would not be the last. Also in attendance were American comedians Jerry Lewis, Phil Silvers and Dick Van Dyke and the writer Roald Dahl, who had penned the hugely successful film's screenplay.

ROYAL VARIETY PERFORMANCE

13 November 1967

The Queen chats to British-American comedian Bob Hope at the London Palladium, where he has just performed in the Royal Variety Performance alongside a star-studded line-up including singers Sandie Shaw, Tom Jones and Val Doonican. Comedians Tommy Cooper, Ken Dodd and Harry Secombe also performed. To meet Her Majesty, Sandie Shaw changed from her stage outfit, saying, 'A mini is fine on stage but I am told it would be more elegant to be presented to the Queen in something a little more special.'

ROYAL ASCOT

June 1968

A happy Queen and Duke of Edinburgh look on as the Prince of Wales waves from their horse-drawn carriage as it passes through the village of Cheapside on the way to the Royal Ascot race meeting. As ever, this year's meeting was as much about what everyone was wearing as it was about the actual racing, especially as it was the year in which the dress code for men was relaxed. Lounge suits were now permitted as well as morning suits, except in the Royal Enclosure, where grey or black morning dress and a top hat were still *de rigeur*.

ROYAL VARIETY PERFORMANCE

10 November 1969

The Queen smiles as she is introduced to the French singer Mireille Mathieu at the London Palladium, performing in the second of her three Royal Variety Performances. To Mademoiselle Mathieu's immediate right is singer-comedian Des O'Connor and on his right is female impersonator Danny La Rue. The Russian-born theatrical impresario Bernard Delfont, on Her Majesty's left, carries out the introductions. Other performers included Roy Castle, Cilla Black, Ginger Rogers, Buddy Rich, Ronnie Corbett, Tom Jones and Herb Alpert and his Tijuana Brass.

WALKABOUT IN THE SEYCHELLES

March 1972

Her Majesty is the recipient of many odd gifts on her travels, such as the seven-year-old bull elephant given to her by the President of Cameroon in 1972 to mark her and the Duke of Edinburgh's Silver Wedding. That same year, she visited the Seychelles, where she was presented with a gift of two tortoises. She is seen here on one of her famous walkabouts, a practice that began in 1970 while she and her husband were visiting New Zealand and Australia. Walkabouts, although an obvious security nightmare, allow the Royal Family to meet as many people as possible.

MURDER ON THE ORIENT EXPRESS PREMIÈRE

November 1974

The Queen is clearly enjoying herself at the première of the film *Murder on the Orient Express*, starring Albert Finney as the Belgian Inspector Hercule Poirot and also featuring an all-star cast of suspects, including Sean Connery, Lauren Bacall, Anthony Perkins, John Gielgud, Michael York, Vanessa Redgrave, Ingrid Bergman and Dame Wendy Hiller. The book from which the film was adapted was written in 1934 by Agatha Christie, who attended the première, aged 84. It would be her last public appearance before her death in January 1976.

ROYAL VARIETY PERFORMANCE

10 November 1975

The Queen greets colourfully dressed members of the KwaZulu Dance Company after a Royal Variety Performance at the London Palladium. The 1975 show featured Bruce Forsyth, Count Basie and his Orchestra, Michael Crawford, Telly Savalas, Charles Aznavour, the cast of BBC Television's 'Dad's Army', Harry Secombe and Vera Lynn. As always, it raised a considerable amount of money for the Entertainment Artistes' Benevolent Fund. Her Majesty is wearing the fabulous 'the Girls of Great Britain and Ireland Tiara', affectionately known as 'Granny's Tiara', as it was given to her by her grandmother as a wedding present.

WELCOME IN NORTHERN IRELAND

August 1977

The Queen disembarks from her first helicopter flight as she arrives at Hillsborough Castle during her first visit in 11 years to troubled Northern Ireland. The visit, part of Her Majesty's Silver Jubilee tour of her kingdom, was surrounded by the most stringent security operation of her reign, with a specially strengthened contingent of 32,000 troops and police on duty. The helicopter was used as it provided the most secure means of transport. During the visit, Her Majesty hosted an investiture and a garden party for several thousand guests and visited the New University of Ulster at Coleraine.

GREETING CROWDS
IN BERLIN

May 1978

Her Majesty the Queen's second visit to West Germany was at the invitation of President Walter Scheel. Her visits to Germany were always somewhat controversial, given the nature of that country's relationship with Britain during the twentieth century, but she is always greeted with an enthusiastic reception, as can be seen in this picture in which a smiling Queen, carrying a bouquet, waves to the cheering crowds as she goes on a walkabout. Immediately to Her Majesty's right can be seen West German Chancellor Helmut Schmidt.

VISIT TO A SCHOOL
IN ABU DHABI

February 1979

Wearing a delightful hat decorated with flowers, the Queen visits Al Khubairat Community School in Abu Dhabi, where she is greeted by hundreds of children waving flags. Her Majesty's tour of the Gulf States lasted 18 days, taking in Kuwait, Qatar, Bahrain, Saudi Arabia, the United Arab Emirates and Oman. As ever on such trips, a great deal of curiosity was expressed in the media about how a female monarch would be treated in Arab countries, but Her Majesty already knew many of the leaders and prominent people she met through their shared love of horse-racing.

VISIT TO THE RED CROSS HEADQUARTERS

April 1980

The Queen and the Duke of Edinburgh pay a visit to the headquarters of the International Red Cross in Geneva, accompanied by the President of Switzerland, Georges-André Chevallaz. The Queen and the Duke's four-day visit to Switzerland, the first official visit by a reigning British monarch, was a triumph, the customary Swiss attention to detail ensuring that everything went like clockwork. In Berne, the capital's famous fountains had been specially gilded for the visit, and in Lucerne, 3,000 screaming, flag-waving schoolchildren lined the Schweizerhofquai.

ROYAL VARIETY PERFORMANCE

23 November 1981

Her Majesty exchanges a joke with Cliff Richard after watching him perform at the 54th Royal Variety Performance. This was the singer's sixth appearance before the Queen and he has performed in 12 Royal Variety Performances to date. Other stars that evening were Jim Davidson, Kenny Lynch, Lenny Henry, Itzhak Perlman, John Inman, Lonnie Donegan, Mike Yarwood, The Searchers, Adam and the Ants, Anita Harris and Jimmy Tarbuck.

GREETING CROWDS
IN KIRIBATI

October 1982

Former British colony the Gilbert Islands are everyone's idea
of what South Pacific islands should look like – swaying palm
trees, golden beaches and azure seas. They became
independent in 1979, taking the name Kiribati, which is
Gilbertese for 'Gilberts'. The Queen and the Duke of
Edinburgh are seen during their visit with recently re-elected
Kiribati President Ieremia Tabai, waving to large, enthusiastic
crowds from the back of a Landrover. They were later treated
to a *tirere*, a rarely seen dance performed by pairs of dancers
wielding percussion sticks.

FEAST IN TUVALU

October 1982

During her tour of the South Pacific, Her Majesty attends a feast in her honour in Tuvalu, one of the tiniest nations on earth. She is wearing a necklace of bone that has been presented to her, as well as a headdress crown of stephanotis flowers. On this, their only visit to Tuvalu, Her Royal Highness and the Duke of Edinburgh were carried around in ceremonial litters. The Queen's official title in Tuvalu is Elizabeth the Second, by the Grace of God, Queen of Tuvalu and of Her Other Realms and Territories, Head of the Commonwealth, emphasizing the island's status as an independent monarchy.

WELCOME IN BRITISH COLUMBIA

March 1983

On Her Majesty's arrival outside City Hall in Victoria, British Columbia, in Canada, four-year-old Erin Johnson presents her with a posy of flowers. This tour of Victoria and Vancouver followed her tour of California and encompassed Victoria, Vancouver, Nanaimo, Vernon, Kamloops and New Westminster. Royal Visits to Canada began in 1786 when the future King William IV, serving in the Royal Navy, visited Halifax and this was the Queen's 15th visit to Canada both as monarch and princess. Her first was in 1951 when she took the place of her ailing father.

WALKABOUT IN KENT

October 1984

The Queen and the Duke of Edinburgh indulge in a walkabout while on a visit to Kent. Their enthusiasm for meeting and talking to people heightened security fears, especially in the face of new threats. Royal Protection Officer Jim Beaton, on Her Majesty's left, knew this only too well. In 1974, as Princess Anne was returning to Buckingham Palace from a charity event, Ian Ball, who suffered from mental health problems, stopped her vehicle on Pall Mall and attempted to kidnap her. Beaton tried to protect the Princess, but his firearm jammed and he was shot. Princess Anne managed to escape and Beaton was awarded the George Cross for his bravery.

ROYAL ASCOT

June 1989

The Queen and Prince Philip arrive at the Royal Ascot race meeting in an Ascot Landau carriage drawn by four Windsor Greys. The landau is a lightweight, four-wheeled, convertible carriage, and this is one of more than 100 carriages in the Royal Collection that is housed at the Royal Mews at Buckingham Palace. These include the remarkable Gold State Coach that has been used for every Coronation since 1821 and the Glass Coach in which Lady Diana Spencer arrived at St Paul's Cathedral for her wedding to the Prince of Wales.

ROYAL VISIT TO ETON COLLEGE

June 1990

The Queen is welcomed by the pupils of Eton College during a 1990 Royal Visit to celebrate the college's 550th anniversary. Founded in 1440 as 'The King's College of Our Lady of Eton besides Wyndsor' by the 19-year-old Henry VI, Eton was modelled on Winchester College and is the second-oldest public school in the country. Numerous princes and future kings both from Britain and from around the world have been educated there, including Her Majesty's grandsons, Princes William and Harry. It has also educated many prime ministers and statesmen, leading it to be described as 'the chief nurse of England's statesmen'.

GREETING CROWDS IN FRANCE

June 1994

Her Majesty the Queen and the Duke of Edinburgh wave to crowds of veterans before attending a service marking the 50th anniversary of the D-Day landings. The Queen and the Duke had arrived on board the Royal Yacht *Britannia* the previous evening to join the gathering of 19 kings, queens, heads of state and leaders of governments. One of the visits made by the Queen and the Duke of Edinburgh was to Bayeux Cemetery, the largest Second World War cemetery of Commonwealth soldiers in France, resting place of 4,648 soldiers, most of whom lost their lives during the Normandy landings.

VISIT TO THE NATIONAL THEATRE, WARSAW

March 1996

The Queen, wearing a white evening gown and 'the Girls of Great Britain and Ireland Tiara', accompanied by the Duke of Edinburgh, attends Jean Dauberval's comic ballet, *La Fille Mal Gardée*, at the National Theatre in Warsaw during her State Visit to Poland as the guest of President Aleksander Kwaśniewski. During the visit, Her Majesty met former President Lech Walesa, delivered a speech in the Polish Parliament and accepted the gift of a piece of the wreckage of an RAF plane shot down over Warsaw in 1944.

MEETING THE SOUTH AFRICAN CRICKET TEAM

October 1997

During a State Visit to Pakistan, the Queen is introduced by captain Hansie Cronje, on her left, to members of the South African cricket team at Rawalpindi Cricket Club in Islamabad during a test match with Pakistan. Her Majesty's 1997 visit was as Head of the Commonwealth. Following the creation of the country after the Partition of India in 1947, King George VI had become Monarch of the Dominion of Pakistan and, on his death, that role was assumed by Her Majesty. When Pakistan became a republic in 1956, the direct link with the British crown was ended, but a connection remained through Pakistan's membership of the Commonwealth.

CONCERT AT THE ROYAL FESTIVAL HALL

12 November 1997

Her Majesty, holding a bouquet of flowers, attends a concert at the Royal Festival Hall in aid of the Royal Academy of Music and Great Ormond Street Hospital. The concert was dedicated to the memory of the Princess of Wales, who had been killed in a car crash in Paris just 10 weeks previously, leading to an unprecedented outpouring of national grief and a certain amount of criticism of the Queen and the Royal Family. The Princess of Wales had been President of Great Ormond Street Hospital.

THE PARENT TRAP PREMIÈRE

9 November 1998

Her Majesty attends the première of *The Parent Trap*, the film selected as the Royal Film Performance for 1998. Curtsying as she meets the Queen is the late British actress Natasha Richardson, while another star of the film, Dennis Quaid, looks on to her left. Behind him can be seen Mr Quaid's wife, the actress Meg Ryan. This was the 52nd film selected for a Royal Film Performance and, as usual, the proceeds from the evening were donated to the Cinema and Television Benevolent Fund.

RE-OPENING OF THE ROYAL OPERA HOUSE

1 December 1999

The current Royal Opera House, home to the Royal Ballet and the Royal Opera, dates back to 1858 and is the third theatre on the site in Covent Garden. By the 1990s it was in serious need of refurbishment and work took place between 1996 and 2000 to turn it into what is claimed to be the most modern theatre facility in Europe. The Queen is seen attending the Opening Celebration, which featured numerous stars of opera and ballet, including singers Placido Domingo and Deborah Polaski and dancers Viviana Durante and Sylvie Guillem.

CASINO ROYALE PREMIÈRE

14 November 2006

It seemed only fitting that the man who had come to the nation's rescue so many times on screen – James Bond, Agent 007 – should be the subject of the 60th Royal Film Performance. *Casino Royale* was the second Bond film to be accorded the honour, *Die Another Day* starring Pierce Brosnan having been selected in 2002. Her Majesty is seen at the Odeon, Leicester Square, meeting the actor Daniel Craig, who was playing the debonair spy for the first time. Also attending the première were Sir Elton John, Dame Shirley Bassey and Sir Richard Branson.

SERVICE AT WESTMINSTER ABBEY

16 November 2011

Her Majesty accepts a posy of flowers as she leaves a service of celebration at Westminster Abbey marking the 400th anniversary of the King James Bible. Described during the service by the Archbishop of Canterbury as 'extraordinary' and of 'abiding importance', the translation was ordered by King James I and VI in 1604 in an attempt to create unity between religious factions. The final editing of the 'Authorized Version' of the King James Bible was completed in the Jerusalem Chamber of the Abbey in 1611 and had an enduring impact on English language and culture throughout the world.

INDEX